T0064559

THE STORM IS CALM

TERRY LEE MCCLAIN

authorHOUSE®

AuthorHouse™
1663 Liberty Drive
Bloomington, IN 47403
www.authorhouse.com
Phone: 1 (800) 839-8640

Published by AuthorHouse 01/28/2015

ISBN: 978-1-4969-6704-6 (sc)
ISBN: 978-1-4969-6703-9 (e)

Scripture quotations marked KJV are from the Holy Bible, King James
Version (Authorized Version). First published in 1611. Quoted from the KJV
Classic Reference Bible, Copyright © 1983 by The Zondervan Corporation.

DEDICATIONS

To my grand-daughter (Ariah), I wish you well at what path you choose in life. Follow your dreams and keep God near and dear to your heart. I love you to the end of the world… And to the lost that want to be found.

Contents

Chapter 1
Today [October 7, 2013(Monday)]

Today is overcast with rain, a slow drizzle. The fall season is in and the trees are starting to barely change colors. Today is a beautiful day even though it is raining. I have learned that every day (by Gods will) is a beautiful day no matter the conditions. Always know that God has given you another day to live by His will and HIS will alone. Therefore, be happy that He has shown you His grace and mercy to allow you another day to live.

Today I am still remembering a friend that was buried yesterday (Mr. Walden Johnson). His sister Gloria allowed me to speak during the remarks section of the service; I was most honored to say remarks for such a friend as Walden (he preferred me to call him Walter). His death was so sudden to me that I still have trouble grasping the reality of the whole matter. One day he left to go to the hospital and days later he was pronounced dead; he never returned home.

He was *Ole School* till the very end. I remember him riding through the neighborhood in his clean car (a 1992 green Lexus with the music blasting). He was laid back and kool. We cut grass and bushes together and we often set on his porch and talked. I knew him well for the past year and a half of his life and he was a real friend. I don't know much about his life before I met him and I despise "Hearsay". I believe that the last state of a man is his best testimony for having lived life and this is what I knew about Walter when he died; He was not on drugs, did not drink alcohol, nor smoked cigarettes. Therefore, if there be anyone to be quick to judge my friend, you must agree with me on one thing: No one living owns a heaven or hell to put anyone in. I will miss Walter and I will never forget the wisdom he left behind for me; he was sixty two when he passed. And from his sudden death I say to you: Love and enjoy what you have right now; stop worrying about what you don't have, because when you leave this world you will carry nothing with you.

Today our government (USA) is shut down. It is embarrassing before the world that the number one country in the world is not functioning because some members of the Senate and House of Representatives are intransigent with our first African- American president (Mr. Obama) and his ideas as to how this country should function for the well fair of the people of the United States of America. It seems to me that if president Obama is smart enough to talk a dictator (Al assad) of Syria into surrendering his chemical weapons without military force, then I believe he is more than qualified to make the right decisions as to how our government should operate for the well fair of the people. I truly believe Mr. Obama and Mr. Biden (vice president) together are in their positions for the well fair of the American people and I truly believe they are guiding our country in the right direction.

Today, I am happy about the life I am living, I am mostly going to lie in bed and rest until the rain stops.

I had my only grand-daughter (Ariah) and her friend Cassidy over last weekend and we had a wonderful time together. I took Ariah to the McDonalds play pin and later to a local park. I even went down the sliding board with her. I haven't been down a sliding board in over thirty- five years. My grand-daughter was tickled to death to be playing with me and to see me come down that sliding board. Later, after going to get doughnuts from Crispy Cream and returning home, her friend Cassidy had come over. We played with Lego building blocks and baby dolls (yea, at 50 years old I had to play with baby dolls) well into the late night hours (they were so happy to have me playing with them). I finally convinced them to lie down for the night and after a long battle at convincing them to go to sleep; they finally lost the battle and fell off to sleep around one o'clock a.m. It was all so much fun. My future wife Deneen just looked on in amazement at the fun we was having. It was moments like those I will never forget. Again, enjoy what you have right now, because Today is all we have, yesterday is gone, and tomorrow is not promised to any of us.

I have come to understand that life is like a roller coaster; it is filled with ups and downs. There is no way around them; you are going to have them throughout your life time. Be strong and pray and know within your heart that Christ will get you through anything. You have to always believe that if God has gotten you this far, then if it is His will; He will keep you until He is ready for you to return to heaven.

I am writing that you might hear my voice and what I am speaking of. I learned a lot from the death of my friend; life truly is like a vapor. You see it one moment and then it is gone. Therefore, always be real about the love you hold for your loved ones; embrace them and keep them near your heart, because in a moment they can be gone.

I bring this story to you at a height in my life that many have not reached. I feel as though I am living the best days of my life and there is no turning back. I reach out to you and say, believe that it is ok to be ok. Always, continue to follow your dreams and except no one's thoughts of you; for you are great and except nothing less.

I am not speaking as though I live in a Rose garden. I am human and I have some problems just like you. We all as a human race have a little something wrong going on in our lives. There is no perfect life anybody human can live. You have problems that are not mine and I have problems that are not yours. The key that opens the door to happiness and inner fulfillment is in your mind and heart. The way you think and feel determines how you deal with the problems and frustrations of life. Therefore, keep your mind sober and be humble in your heart then the desires of your heart will follow.

Today, there is still many bizarre crimes going on in this country (USA); far too many. I wrote about these things in my first book called "I Hunt" and the trends of violent and strange crimes continue. The latest trend is the killings of small infants (One, Two, and Three years old) by way of domestic violence. I just do not understand these types of people. These live in boyfriends and baby sitters are constantly in the news for harming or killing innocent children. People! Be careful as to whom you allow to take care of your children (if you really love them). I am beginning to question the morals of the parents of these innocent babies. If it is a boyfriend problem, seek HELP and if it is a baby sitter problem, get another one. Do not just reach your child out to danger. The police and social workers are put in their positions for a purpose; USE THEM. Another trend of violence is the horrific and senseless school killings. I truly believe that since the schools took out the Ten Commandments and prayer God has sent this evil spirit upon them. You can believe me or not, but view the evidence and the number of these crimes then see if you can honestly agree with me. I hope and pray that the people running schools will see that the world cannot function without some kind of spiritual belief and understanding. And bring back prayer and The Ten Commandments.

Finally, in March of 2013 in Brunswick GA; two boys age seventeen and fourteen attempted to rob a woman that was walking her sixteen month old baby along the side walk in a stroller. She resisted, saying she didn't have any money. One of the two boys shot her in the leg and went around to the front of the stroller and shot the baby in the face; killing it.

America, are you going to wake up as adults and control the youth you are growing up? Hey! Kids fourteen and seventeen have no business carrying guns and harboring such evil in their hearts. It all makes me wonder as to what kind of society my four year old grand-daughter is growing into. All I can say is; parents please wake up. The whole incident was so senseless. I felt empty inside and could only shake my head. Where are the parents in cases like this? (I am starting to feel as though the parents should also be charged with something when their children commit the above type of horrific crime.)

Chapter 2

Order

The understanding I have acquired for this life is that God has a plan in place and He placed Jesus Christ to be the Head of His plan. Therefore, there is an Order to this life. God controls everything about the Order as to how this world works. See how the trees stand still, the animals exist for their purpose, and the oceans send their waves to the shore at a constant rate. Yes, God controls the good and the bad. My brother Roydell once told me that it was amazing how God controls everything at one time, all the time. Think on this: When Adam ate of the forbidden fruit and saw that he was naked. God asked him saying, how did you know you were naked? See, God told Adam & Eve not to eat from the tree of knowledge because He said they would become aware of good and evil. Therefore, I would have to say, that God had already planned to put evil in place. My knowledge runs deep and to propel your mental ability to think on high levels such as these; I must be real as to the reality that I perceive and then you can't say that I distorted the truth. If you think the above sayings are distorted then open your mind and truly look at the reality around you and the forth coming verse: *From Isaiah 45: 7, God is speaking and says: I form the light and create darkness, I make peace and create evil, I the Lord do all these things.* I spoke of this verse in my first book as a question to my readers and now I will reveal the answer. See, everything you are going through (good or evil) or have already come through is directly related to the verse I mentioned above. God controls the good and evil about your life and only you can guide the Order that God has put in place for your life. It is up to you as to what you want for your life.

Hey! We all as a human race have something that we are attached to; whether it be food, hunting, gambling, sex, drugs and so many other things. Always know that no matter what you're attached to, you are not out of the Order of where God wants you to be. So, keep the faith that you have now, pray every day, and trust in God and the Lord Jesus Christ and you can overcome any problems that enter your life. Where you are right now in life is no coincidence or accident. We all are placed in the Order of Gods plan. If you always keep in your mind that every moment you live you are in Gods will and acknowledge that it is His will that you take your next breath; then no matter your problems, God will pull you through and get you to the next stage of His plan. Therefore, never worry about the things that are wrong in your life, look at the good things around you and that is in you and soon your life will appear as the beauty of the sun coming up from behind the ocean. Trust me on this one. Life is the most beautiful gift you will ever receive; embrace it with all the strength you have and enjoy it. Because, you were given this one gift one time; enjoy it for there is no more.

Chapter 3
Youth

I remember the days when I was just a youth. My life was most grand. I grew up in a neighborhood called Ebenezer. Ebenezer is just West of Gastonia North Carolina off of highway 74 in Kings Mtn North Carolina. I was young with plenty of energy. I remember when we (my brothers and neighborhood friends) use to play football in other neighbors yards (in which I see none of today). It is sad that technology has taken away the real child and produced in house video children (Xbox, TV, and the new age music). It seems that all children do today is stay in the house and destroy their talents by using products and ideas made by other people. The kids today are not using their God given talents (and we wonder why there are not any jobs).

Oh, back to the days of playing football in Ebenezer. We use to play all day; nearly every Sunday like the NFL. When I say we I mean twenty or thirty kids from the families in and around the neighborhood. The McClains, Bells, Parkers, Oates, Womics, Adams, Odoms, Byers, Herndons, Hagers, Smiths, Hoods, and others. We even use to travel to different neighborhoods in downtown Kings Mtn North Carolina and play different groups of kids. We also use to play in West Shelby North Carolina in a field that was once a closed down school's football stadium. We had so much fun and it seems as though no one ever got injured (seriously). Believe it or not, we played full contact football with no pads or helmets. Again, it was so much fun! I will never forget those days.

We use to play a lot of basketball also. I was never a good basketball player though. I just never did get the layup move in place and even to this day I struggle to make a good layup. Oh well, maybe one day somebody will show me the best way to make a simple layup.

I also remember the days of picking strawberries. We use to pick them by the gallons. The Lineberger family owned the strawberry fields and we picked for them at a dollar and quarter a gallon. We often ate more than we picked. I believe a kid from every family in Ebenezer at least once picked strawberries for the Linebergers. The Linebergers still own strawberry fields to this day in Stanley North Carolina. In the 70's a dollar and quarter per gallon was a lot of money to a 7 or 8 year old kid. Sometimes, one kid could pick 10 to 20 gallons in one day. We stayed at the strawberry fields all day. It was hot and yet fun. Those were the days when you could look across a field and see the heat rays rising toward the sky.

Especially; when it was hay hauling season. Even hauling hay was fun; (sometimes). I don't remember ever seeing snakes and that is rare, especially around strawberries and hay. I believe to this day that the Divine was ever present and watching over us. Also, I believe that football, basketball, hauling hay, and picking strawberries made us tough like the men we are today (Myself, six brothers, and old neighborhood friends). And, you just don't see these kinds of activities going on today. It truly makes me wonder where this country is going with the little ones.

Chapter 4
Stars Shine

The adult life is mostly a good one, although it comes with highs and lows (it is just the way life is). I tell the young, do not try to grow up to quickly; cherish your youth with joy for there will come a day in your life perhaps when you can look back and see just how valuable being young really was. Therefore, the adult life is not as fun as it seems to be and you will have good days and bad days. What I am trying to say is being an adult is not rewarding all the time. I am not being negative, I just want to try and get a fact across to you. Kids these days want to rush to become an adult and really don't know what their growing into. They don't know that they're only one bad decision away from a life time of trouble with the law. I could surly speak of many other things that they're not aware of.

I am fifty years old and most of my desires for life when I was young (12 to 25) have not been fulfilled. Today, it is not easy being an adult. Your life will develop to become more and more complex. I will give you just a small amount of a lot that is going on in my own life right now. You will deal with problems such that you will struggle to solve them (relationships and how to keep a dollar in your pocket). I now deal with several complex problems. I am not in the best position financially and I struggle with the fact that as an author it is not easy to sell my books as an African American writer. See, Jealousy is the main problem among black people that keeps us from reaching our highest potential. Jealousy among blacks came from the days of slavery and I will never think otherwise (that's just my theory). And to this day in time (the year 2014) nothing has changed much. I will always do my best to change this characteristic among my people though; even if it takes me alone, one day at a time.

I will solve my life problems one at a time though (it's the only way), because I never ever give up on anything I believe in strong enough. My time will come as well as yours if you believe in yourself and Jesus strong enough. My position in life will change soon. I have no doubts.

In my first book "I Hunt" I wrote of the beauty of my life at that time. My inner man still feels the same. I mostly write to the young of this generation that I may give them *Hope*. Hope to lead a better life in a seemingly bad world. I also speak to all ages. Never give up *Hope*. Therefore, the above was to let you know that no matter what you are dealing with in your life, don't give in or give up. You must believe in yourself. Thus, *Stars Shine*! You don't have to be on TV or in front of cameras all the time to be a star. My days are spent *Trying*. Trying to create a better life for myself and the people in my life I truly care about. I pray and ask God for nothing. For the scriptures speak of what Jesus said concerning prayer. (Paraphrasing) He basically said, when you pray say the Lord's Prayer, asking God for nothing for

God already knows what you need and go in to your closet (somewhere private or where no one can see you pray) and pray the Lord's Prayer and what is seen by God in darkness will show openly in due time. Therefore, stop asking God for materialistic things (cars, money, houses, jobs and expensive boats). God will give you yours in His time frame. My motto today is such: If God brings me forth to live another day then I will *Try* my very best; because I know nothing is up to me. I always acknowledge that it is by God's will that I continue to exist and have my soul and it's by His will only. I feel if I always acknowledge that I am in His will every day I live then I believe everything else I need in this life will come to me. I suggest the above to you also. I write to give hope to the people that so desire to be more than they are right now in this life. Therefore, I tell you again that Stars Shine! Because God really wants us to prosper (to have nice things) and He gives these things to you and I according to how we live for Him. Thus, *you and I are Stars* and before God we are suppose to Shine.

I am proud to have lived in the era of Stars like Mr. Jackson, Jordan, Bird, Ali, "Magic" Johnson, Roddman, Mckale, and so many others. And so are you a Star. I believe that we as mankind are the creation of a creator that placed us all on a chess board and He moves us how He pleases. We are like actors on stage in a play or in a movie. You just have to see the star you are from within. You must believe that it's ok to be ok. You don't have to live down on yourself or be ashamed to do well because you think others will be jealous of you. Hey! It's ok to own a BMW, Lexus or Jaguar. It's ok to buy a new house and have several thousand dollars in the bank. God gave you and I a life to live; Live it to the fullest and care less of the ones that are jealous of you. Again, always care less of what someone else thinks of you. Thus, as the Star you also are; "Shine"! Sparkle like the rays leaping from the sun. Therefore, I have looked at my past and present life and noticed that I have not reached my true potential, because I was always caught up in the thought of what others thought of me. I have held myself down; myself alone. I came to the conclusion though that it's ok to be ok and that's the way I live now. I believe if it's ok for the next man to own a yacht, pontoon boat or bass boat; then it is ok for me to own one too. The problem today is that too many people are concerned with what Angie and Sam are doing and not concentrating on what self can do or need to be doing to reach their own full potential or expectations. Therefore, be the Star that you are and Shine!

CHAPTER 5

THE SERMON OF TERRY

Titled: "Reach up for the hand of God"

The sun cast its rays for a reason; so
shall the Lord be glorified in every season.

Quote by: Terry Lee McClain

I come to you, in honor of our Lord and savior Jesus Christ.
I will come from Psalm 116:1-2. I Love the Lord, because
he hath heard my voice and my supplications. Because he
hath inclined his ear unto me, therefore will I call upon him
as long as I live.

My message is such: "Reach up for the hand of God". I
come to you because I have hope in you as well as all others.

I ran into a man several months ago ("Bobby" Reid).
It seems as though nobody in the neighborhood and
surrounding area found anything much good to say about
this man. (Like I've said before; I despise "Hearsay"). We
began to hang out during the day; doing odd jobs together
for different people. He would find the oddest of jobs. I

call him "One Job Bob", because he would find a job and it would take him all day to do it. We hauled junk to the scrap yard mostly; spread mulch, and plant flowers. I have to give it to him; the man knows how to make an honest dollar. I began to like this man as a friend and I began to wonder why other people talked so negative about this man. I wondered why everyone talked down on this man. You know, Jesus hung among the worst of people and my belief is that He did so in the hope of being a good example that someone would follow. See, you never know when you may be a good example for someone else. That's why I never look down on anyone, because you never know what good may be in a person or whom you may need to call on for help one day.

Today, it seems as though people are quick to judge others and not look at their own faults. No one wants to see the good in somebody any more. Believe it or not; we all have faults and bad ways. The point I am trying to make is that you cannot always know a person just by the bad things you have heard about him/her. You have to sometimes open your mind and concentrate on the good you see in a person. We all have a past! Look at yours sometime and see if you remember anything bad in it.

I tell you, I'm hot right now! The spirit of the Lord is beneath me and the heat is rising! When it seems as though no one can see any good in you, reach up for the hand of God! I tell you, when Jona was in the belly of a whale, he reached up for the hand of God! When Moses was at the edge of the Red Sea, he reached up for the hand of God! When Daniel was in the lion's den, he reached up for the hand of God! Yea, when Shadrach, Meshach, and

Abed-nego were in the fiery furnace, they reached up for the hand of God and were delivered!

I tell you, When you're at your worst point and don't know how to go on, reach up for the hand of God! When drugs and alcohol have taken over your life, reach up for the hand of God! No matter what you're going through, reach up for the hand of God! He will deliver you!

When I wandered in the heat of the sun of Florida in 1990 for three days; with no money and hungry, I reached up for the hand of God! When I had a heart attack at age forty two in 2006, I reached up for the hand of God! Heyyyy! I Thank God through Jesus Christ I will be fifty one on June 18, 2014. I've had many situations where I didn't know how I would get through them, I reached up for the hand of God and He heard me.

To this day I stand bold as a man and I know I would not be here if I didn't reach up for the hand of God. His mercy and grace never changes. He is the same God today as he was in the days of Pharaoh. I tell you! His love for His children never changes.

I have spoken unto you that you might open your eyes and hear with your ears; trust in the Lord, and love Him all the days you have left to live. He will answer your prayers if you trust in Him. Again, I say, reach up for the hand of God!

Like I said earlier about "Bobby", pray for this man and perhaps he too will reach up for the hand of God one day. Love thy neighbor as thyself. That's why I say, never put others down, because you never know when you too might have to reach up for the hand of God. Before you put a person down; pray for that person that God will lift that person up just as He have lifted you up in times past.

Again, my mission is always to give you hope. Hope that you too one day might see the true power of God.

Take in mind, I am not a pastor. I am just a Christian trying to be a better man each day through Jesus Christ. I wrote the above, because if I was a preacher it is what I would preach to a congregation. Also, I have read the Holy Bible (original King James Version) completely through twice and I wanted to see how I would do if I was a preacher. How do you think I done? Therefore, continue to pray for me as I do for you and all others. And continue to reach up for the hand of God. Amen!

Chapter 6
Straight Talk

It is Tuesday February 11, 2014 and our second winter storm is upon us. The snow is slowly falling. The snow flacks fall in unison; floating to the earth like the feathers of a dove, landing softly, and covering the ground like covering a child at night to sleep. We rarely see snow fall to a large degree as this in the area of Mt. Holly North Carolina.

My mode is relaxed and subtle. I embrace the feeling that a cascading snow fall gives me. It really is soothing to my soul.

The conditions are supposed to change for the worst tomorrow. Tomorrow is to bring more snow and perhaps the most we have seen in this area in over ten years.

I love to write on days like this. It frees my mind of the general stresses of life (for we all deal with something every day).

I hope by the end of this book you will feel the same as I do now (very calm inside). My purpose of writing this book is to reveal to you a new outlook on the life you now possess. I hope you are relaxed enough to continue reading my work.

I look again at my past and I feel relieved that I am now by those days. You know, you can get through anything if the desire is strong enough. I have lived some rough days as an adult. The drinking, drugs (very little), homelessness, and seemingly countless stays in jails. I have lived through days that had no direction, nothing to do, and nowhere to go. I have had the feeling of not wanting to see the next day come (The worst feeling I believe a man can ever feel). I have been in jails in Shelby NC, Gastonia NC, Charlotte NC, Durham NC, and an overnight stay in Winston Salem NC. Also, three prison stays; for DWI and snatching money out of cash registers (all foolishness). I know and believe today that I was carrying out these foolish acts because I didn't have a normal teenage life. I started working in a cotton mill full-time at age sixteen and going to college full-time; leaving school and going directly to work. And due to the hectic schedule I didn't have time to be a regular teenager. Therefore, in my late twenties I started to commit crimes that teenagers are known for.

I no longer live those type of days and will always pray that it is the Lord's will that I never see again days such as those. During those times I truly never wanted to hurt anyone and thank God through Jesus Christ that I never did (physically). Again, I was only coping the best I could with a terrible position I had foolishly put my life in. I really cannot imagine harming another human being to the point of serious injury or death. I cherish all manner of life. I didn't give it and I feel I have no right to take it from anyone. Out of all the criminal activity I have spoken of above; I feel as though it was never a part of the person I really am inwardly as a human being and I will always feel this way. And, anyone I may have harmed in anyway; I am here to say that _I am sorry_. I am really a very humble person and love the existence of life with a passion.

Therefore, the key to living a better life is to change. Again, Change (make better decisions). No matter how hard it may seem or the odds against you; you can do it. You must look deep within your inner being and separate the good from the bad. I often look back at my childhood and my mother's life at that time. My moma (Sally Ann Ross-McClain) was a caring woman. She hardly ever went anywhere without us (myself and my brothers). She always cooked for us and kept us clean. And speaking of cooking, my moma can cook to this day food that taste so good it will make you want to slap the jump out of a monkey. I can always appreciate her for taking care of us even though she had her own struggles (drinking alcohol). She was and still is the model mom though and I love her to the end of the world. Today, she has been alcohol free for over thirty-six years. Thus, I know a person can change if she/he has the desire to do so.

Also, I look back at the times when my relatives (Ross, McClain, and Wray) and only God knows the many other people that use to gather with them in West Shelby North Carolina in the 70's. They gathered mostly on the weekends to gamble, drink (alcohol), and fight. They would drink and fight; makeup and drink some more. We (the kids) would play in and around the streets until a fight broke out and that was often over the whole town. I will never forget those days and what they mean to me today as an adult.

West Shelby was like the Western towns you see in the movies. Not one house was level nor was a level ever seen during their construction. All the houses in this town had to of been built by the naked eye or the drunken eyes of the builders. Also, it seemed that all the adults in this town were either on beer, wine, or pot; my aunts, uncles, and parents included. Today I truly do embrace the memories of those days and always will. It was truly an interesting and fun experience. Furthermore, I will never forget my grandmother (Dorenda Ross). We all called her moma. She was paralyzed on one side by a stroke. She never gave in to her condition and never gave up on her children. I loved her something awful. She often asked me to massage her foot (the one that was paralyzed) and to cook her food that she really was not suppose to have (pork products). She would have me to cook her eggs, bacon, or sausage. It was our secret because her children didn't want her to have these products. She never gave up hope of walking normal again. (I believe I got the determination, will power, and patience I have today from her). She was a beautiful human being with the strength of five lions. I miss her to this day. Also, she would send me to the store with food stamps and no matter how much she had (little or a lot) she always told me to get myself something. She too was a great role model. She also truly believed in the Lord and I will always pray that if anybody goes to heaven; she did. Rest in peace moma; *always.*

As an adult now I can truly say I learned a lot from those days and I can see the changes my family members have made since then. Again, I know today that change must occur in one's life in order to make it better (only if you desire a better life). I have witnessed the *Change* in nearly all of my family members of that time. Today, most of my aunts, uncles, and my moma live an alcohol and drug free life (some; complete abstinence) and I am proud of every one of them. I know now as an adult that it was by desire, determination, and the true will of God that my relatives changed their lives.

Thus, you must believe in something beyond yourself (I prefer God and Jesus Christ) then you must look deep within yourself and believe in who you really believe you are. Then the *Change* will come to the light. You can begin right now; no matter your condition, predicament, or status in life right now. You can change right now. You have to believe that you are no better or worse off than the next man/woman. I believe that the rich man is no more important than the poor man, because the rich man was created too. To me, President Obama is no more important as a human being as the man holding up the homeless sign at the intersection. That is just the way I look at it all. You are important too if you have the desire to *Change. Change* must occur.

I am writing this book in order that you may begin to see your life as an open rose. Gather yourself and begin to believe that your life is just as important as the next person. For, *Right Now* and the rest of what you do for your life is the only thing that matters. I write as the material flows through my mind and I am coming to you with *Straight Talk*.

Even now as the snow falls during a winter storm; I feel within like the sun is shining on a cloudless and blue sky day. Therefore, remember always that only by the Mercy and Grace of the Creator of all living things is the purpose you still live and have your being.

Chapter 7
On Course

The days of my life thus far have been a series of ups and downs. I am happy today that I have endured the downs. You know, the race is never decided by how swift one begins, but by the faith it takes to endure to the end. I rarely look back at the mistakes I have made in the past, because nothing of the past can define who you choose to be at the present. I firmly believe that a person can choose at any moment to be what he/she really wants to be. I am saying; you don't have to be a wine-o, drug addict, or alcoholic if you don't want to be. I look at most people and I realize that there are a lot of people that don't have serious mental problems (knowing right from wrong) and know how to make the right decision. I am one that has made the adjustments in my life that proves anybody can redirect their life for a better status in society and be a productive member thereof. For one, I know I am no better than anybody else and feel boldly that there is nobody better than me. See, sometimes people tend to think that their status defines the worth of a person. I truly feel sorry for the people that judge others only by status and their past and never acknowledge the accomplishments and positive contributions to society of other people and family members. They only see their own worth and accomplishments as the corner stone of life. I have a message for these people; the same rope (family and friends) you used to climb to your status may one day be the same rope you need to hold on to while falling.

See, I read books and people. You most likely read for entertainment and I applaud you. I read people mostly. And I have learned to discern the good/bad in people. I found that life is less stressful for me if I learn the attitudes and mental moods of other people.

See, you can believe me or not; God created us all and we all have a past. Again, look at your own past and see if you have lived a perfect life or have not had to call on someone for their help. Again, I firmly believe that the past of person doesn't define his/her entire life time or define what a person can ultimately become (lawyer, doctor, engineer, politician, etc…). We all have sinned before God, bleed the same color of blood, and discharge waste the same way. Sure, I have been to prison and been homeless too, but none of that matters to me today; it didn't stop me from continuing my quest for happiness and building a better life for myself. Thus far I have (a Mechanical Engineering degree, full benefits from my time in the Navy, a beautiful grand-daughter, a son as an aspiring Rapper named META#4, a beautiful girlfriend of fifteen years, author of my second book and many other accomplishments). Today, I rarely focus on my past, because the past can only affect your present state if you allow it to. Plus, I don't have time to focus totally on my past, because I know right now and if it's the Lord's will that I live well into the future; the chance and opportunity can come that can make my past look like the changing of time (here in a moment and gone forever). Therefore, I can care less of what someone else thinks of me. For I know *Jesus Christ* is ever in front of me and guiding my life in the direction that *He* has already chosen for me and there is nothing anyone can say or do to stop *His* plan for me.

Therefore, I am on course. My life at this point in time is like a ship drifting smoothly across a calm sea. See, you must begin to see the world and the people in it from within yourself. To view existence for the natural beauty the Creator intended. I will always believe that there is a unique kind of beauty in everything that exists. I tell you, begin to know that your life is on course also. Nothing is out of place. The Creator of all things has you right where He wants you to be. It's up to you and you alone to create a better situation for yourself. I heard someone say once; that if you are driving a car toward a concrete barrier and take your hands off the steering wheel expecting God to grab it. You are mistaken. Yep, you will crash. Opportunity and the chance to live a better life are not going to come and jump in your lap like a cat. I firmly believe that you must help the Creator help you.

If it is addiction, help yourself. If it is financial trouble, help yourself. If it is a domestic problem, help yourself. God will help you with any problem, but you must create the desire within to want His help. Fix your ways and you will see better days. Take in your mind, my life is not perfect; I have only made some necessary adjustments that give me comfort. My peace and happiness are in place because of the adjustments I have made in my life. See, I have been on top and through the bottom; and only by the Mercy and Grace of God do I now still live. No matter your situation right now. I understand, relate, and can sympathize with you in your current predicament. I am telling you right now that any situation or trouble you are going through can change. I don't care what it is. *You* can get through it.

Always remember, fancy cars, money, big houses, and expensive boats can't bring you happiness. By humbleness within, presenting yourself as respectful toward others, acknowledging the successes of others, and belief in a Creator of all things; then you will find peace and happiness and the material things will follow for you to enjoy. Again, whatever you are faced with right now; *you* can get through it. If I can do it; then I feel that you can also.

Keep your head up and defeat your situation and know that you are on course with the plan God has put in place for your life. Forget your past and begin a better future for yourself and your loved ones. I am steering into port and know for sure I am on time and on course with the Almighty God of my understanding.

CHAPTER 8
I AND META#4

The greatest gift from God to me thus far in my life is that my only son (Philip Austin McClain) is headed in the right direction with his life. His artist name is META#4 and as of June 5, 2014 he released his first album entitled (P.O.V.). I listened to it a night or so ago and all I could say was (an AWESOME project). I say to the music world (another genius knocks at the door). He wrote all the lyrics to all the songs. He is a *Rapper* for sure. And take in; this is not a mixed tape. All the songs are his original work. In this explosive array of songs he truly gives you his P.O.V. (point of view). He is twenty-six and gives you the voice of a flow master to describe the ups and downs in his life thus far. I really listened to the song called P.O.V. and I want him to know that; son I am sorry when I was not there for you at the worst points in your life. Again, I am sorry.

I and Meta#4 are one. We have a beautiful relationship and our visions and goals for life are set in place like a brick mason sets the brick. We both are striving to reach the greatest potential at our craft (him in music and I in writing). That's how I describe us as being one. Our quest is not all about money or materialistic things. We are more concerned about getting our voices to you. We are destined to bring forth the voices that will express some of the greatest potentials the mind can reach. We hope to express the inner most skills God has blessed us with. We believe also that if we reach the highest potential of our crafts; the materialistic things and money will follow.

Again, in his music he expresses his ups and downs in life thus far. I and his mother (Anita) broke up after six years of marriage when he was about one and a half. After the break up I was in and out of his life (not by choice) and I never totally neglected him. I tell him now; son I never forgot you and I gave my portion (financially) to help support you along the way. I still posses the financial records to prove my claim. Therefore, our quest continues now as *One* and the past is gone (unchangeable). We have an awesome relationship today and that is all that will ever matter to me. He has given me a very unique grand-daughter (Ariah Melody McClain) that means the world to me and every day I give thanks to the *Good Lord* for them both. I am very proud of them both. Also, I am proud that my grand-daughter's mother (Sheree) and my son made the decision to let her carry our last name. You know, in today's time many break ups are occurring and can get very messy. I am thankful to God that the recent break up of my son and my grand-daughter's mother was not messy. They both have seemingly moved on to different relationships and all seems well. (The young I tell you) I will support my son's decisions and choices no matter whom he's with. I was young too once and had to make difficult decisions. And all I can say now for the above situation is (O'Well) and let the Lord's will be done.

I and META#4 talk here and there fairly often and I get to see my grand-daughter at will. It all gives me a warm heart feeling and I am happy for that. He doesn't know that I am writing about him as of now and I hope he is not disappointed about my writings. *I love you son* and my best wishes toward your coming successes. And I am ecstatic about the path in life you are choosing. My hope is that more young people will choose the same positive path.

Chapter 9
My Crew

The life I live today is going quite well and I am happy. Happiness comes in different forms. My happiness comes from having good people around me and *trying* to make the right decisions for my future. I give all the credit to the Almighty God through Jesus Christ and my crew. Take in mind, I don't live on top of a cake glazed over with perfection and nearly all families have areas of dysfunction. My family history consists of the McClain's (living around Kings Mtn NC and Linconton NC) and the Ross's (living around Shelby NC, Grover NC, and Kingstown NC).

I now reside in Mt. Holly NC with my future wife (Deneen) of fifteen years and her two children (DJ and Denisha). I can't envision myself with anyone else right now; for I have come to realize that all women are basically the same. The same problems you have with one will be the same or worse with another. That's just the way I see it. (If you have a good woman and know that within yourself; you may as well keep her).

My mother (Sally A. McClain) resides in Kings Mtn NC. I am dedicating this chapter to my living family members and deceased ancestors, because at some point in your life (doing good or bad) you're going to need a family members help. I love every member of both sides of my family and the friends I have picked up along the way in my life. I don't get to see a lot of my family members on the McClain side for whatever reason, but I continue to pray that soon we can become more associated. Therefore, I wish to acknowledge the primary people that have had a positive influence thus far in my life to this day (my crew).

My fiancée Deneen of whom has been a tremendous supporter of any project I pursue, my son Philip (META#4) of whom is a rapping and song writing genius, my grand-daughter Ariah (my heart and soul) and her mother Sheree, my mother Sally Ann Ross- McClain, my brother Anthony (my true buddy and friend) and his family (wife Shante, "AJ", Mellinia, and Miata), Duriel (of whom I hold a deep respect toward for the family man he has become) and his family ("Little Man", Cassidy, and wife Crystal), my brother Roydell (of whom is a true provider for his family)and his family (wife Karen, "punkin", and Kendrick) in Asheville NC, James and Alberta of Mt. Holly NC. Again, this is my crew and I love you.

To the deceased and my ancestors: My deddy (Robbie Lee McClain), my grand-paw Andrew McClain and grand-maw Beatrice, my grandmother (Dorenda) and grand-paw Eddie Ross, uncle "JP", my uncle Randolph Ross (an outstanding track star in high school) of whom begat a son (Dywane) that competed at the Olympics in the early 2000's in track& field, my uncle (Rudolph "Uncle Ruddy" Ross) of whom always wanted to go to Hawaii and said, when he got off the plane he would have a weed eater in his hands (to cut the grass skirts off of the Hula dancers), my uncle Roach, my uncle Bill Ross, my uncle Robert Lee Ross, and my aunt Minnie Mae Ross Montgomery (of whom once made a macaroni and cheese dish with spaghetti noodles) it was truly funny, because I had never seen it attempted before, my uncle Paul McClain and his wife Rosie "aunt Rosie", uncle George McClain, aunt Mae Charles Wray-Ross, my first cousin Pam Ross, Mae Helen Ross-Lane, and my two sisters (*Connie Mae and Julie Mae*), my cousins Enslow and Winslow McClain of whom was twins (of whom never seemed to be troubled by anything and always displayed positive attitudes). These were my close ancestors and I will never forget them. Rest in peace; *Always.* The above ancestors have truly helped shape my life (in one form or another) and my love for having been in the presence of most of these people runs deeper than the sea.

To the living: which of whom I consider my true friends and family. And if there's someone I fail to mention I mean no disrespect. First, my crew on the McClain side; my other six brothers (Roger, Roydell, Timmy, Ronnie, Charles, and Anthony) It is said that my deddy had outside children; I don't know for sure and I could care less at this point in my life. I only claim the above as my brothers and to me it will always stay as such. For I loved my deddy and *slander and hearsay I detest.* It is seven of us *men* and we're all still living. It is an amazing blessing from God. Second, on the Ross side; Doren and Danny (my first cousins), Keith Ross, Bill Jr. Ross, uncle Bobby Ross of whom is an aspiring actor and play writer of biblical material, uncle Woodrow Ross

"Fire-ball", and uncle Ricky Starns, Bryant Starns and his family, my aunts (Annie Mae, Margret "Duck", and Doris). Third, the friends that I have been around within the last few years: Bobby "One job Bob", Pop, Jack, Danny, Julius, James, Flip, Buck, and a few others.

I say to the younger generation, learn to know your family members and real friends, because there will come a day in your life that will have you to call on somebody. And, you can search the world over when things get really tough; but these are the ones that will truly be there to lift you up. Trust me.

You will also have rejections from your very own family members and they will talk about you and put your name in the dirt. Therefore, always strive to do right by all men/ women and whatever situation you run into you will have *someone* in place to help you (some family and friends).

Again, Jealousy runs deep among the African American people in this nation (USA) and it saddens me to the core of my soul and someday I pray we can *let it go*; but reality is real no matter how difficult it is to understand sometimes. The other races are not much different; but I do see the trend among my people. Therefore, beware of whom you deal with, because believe me (everybody is not for you toward your goals and successes). And when you sense that someone is jealous of you; set your goals and aspirations even higher. Again, learn and get to know who your family members are.

The above is a general run down of my family and friends and deceased ancestors and as I have mentioned before: You are my crew and I love you.

Chapter 10
I Am Not a Saint

The life I live today is a pleasant one. Since I finally got my full benefits from the Veterans Administration I tend to take life for what it is (sometimes difficult to deal with and beautiful to live; all at the same time). I live one day at a time and never struggle with what happened yesterday. I get up most mornings around 5:30 a.m. (because that's when my girlfriend gets up for work), get organized and head outside. I sit under a huge shade tree in the front yard and gather my thoughts for the day and material to write while *smoking coffee and drinking cigarettes*. (I am not trying to influence or disrespect the young). I just believe in the chemical makeup of a man/woman and not so much in what the people and doctors say. Take in mind; I am not trying to justify my habits. I just believe that it will always be up to God as to how you leave this world. For we all have something we do that doesn't always please everyone else. I truly believe that whatever habits and diseases you have or have obtained; they came here with you. All you can do is pray and hope to make certain adjustments or change your way of doing things.

I go through the day as though I was taking a walk in the park. I tend to take on time as I go through it. I have good days and bad days (feelings wise), but I am always approachable. I rarely concern myself with the past and don't depend too much on the future. For, there is no promise you will be alive tomorrow and the right now is already a hand full.

This poem was written for a friend of mine that had a loved one that died and it is how I view the entire existence of mankind (male and female). The poem is called *"For Us ALL IT IS THE SAME"* and goes as such:

We come. We embark on a journey. Some are long, many are short. Along the way we laugh and we play; we struggle with something almost every day. At the end Death shall come and the soul he will claim… For us all it is the same.

I have likened life to that of a basketball game. It is near the end; the clock reads 00:03 and you are given the chance for the shot to win. The inbound pass is in, you have the ball, you dribble and take the shot, the buzzer sounds, and the crowd erupts into a thunderous roar. You won the game! The other team is heartbroken due to the loss. Life will always be a win or lose game… For us all it is the same.

Our journey through life can be the shot that won the game. Thus, for a loved one; when the clock reads 00:00 because the soul Death came to claim. "Rejoice" with great joy for that loved one and the next game in heaven. Where Jesus Christ is the Head Official and the clock reads "Forever You Will Remain". Again, I say "Rejoice" and Stand firm by the Faith you proclaim… For us all it is the same.

Written & Arranged by: Terry Lee McClain (1/30/2012)

Therefore, I am not a saint. But I believe in the Father, the Son, and the Holy Ghost beyond all doubt. I truly believe that Jesus Christ was sent to earth by God himself and was among us in the flesh, lived a sinless life, and died upon the cross for the remission of our sins. Yes, I have sinned as we all have. Yours are no bigger than mine and mine are no bigger than yours. Also, a little sin is the same as a lot. That is just the way I see it and one day we will all be held accountable. I have changed a lot of my ways and the way I think. I no longer carry on with the foolishness of the streets (running out of stores with beer, taking money out of cash registers and running, drinking alcohol to the point of soberness, doing drugs with unknown people, and sleeping in unknown places) I live in reality today and that is where I want to stay. I want to overshadow my past and build a brighter future for myself and my loved ones.

The way to a better life style is to change your ways and the way you think. It is a process and will take time. It won't happen overnight. Take your time and develop a new manner as to how you conduct your life and the change for the better that you desire will come. Trust me on this one. I live today sober minded and drug free. I neither have the time nor the desire to return to the streets. For I learned from pure experience that the very loved ones (that really love you) you run from out into the streets are the same people you return to, because the cycle of the street life is always going to be the same; you hang out with people that care nothing for you, you spend all your money, and wake up the next morning with nothing (not even a cigarette or enough money to get a cup of coffee). That is living in sin and there is nothing fun about waking up to such a condition. It is sad.

I have spoken the above because I don't want you to have to travel down the same road that I have in the past. I am writing to the young people and to anyone that may be caught in such a cycle and want a better life for themselves.

Again, my days are not lived in a bed of rose pedals. I still struggle with a few habits (smoking cigarettes and mismanaging money) and I will continue to pray that one day by God's will I will become more stable at handling these types of habits.

Thus, no matter how big your house is or the type of car you drive; one day you too will be no more and the material things will be left behind. For us all it is the same. Therefore, learn to love your family members and friends as you love yourself. Respect toward others and compassion for others condition can ultimately cover many sins. Believe me; life on earth will never be all about you or me.

Chapter 11
Moving Forward

I often reflect on the days gone by and where I have come from. The thought of going through many of those days is sickening to me today. I look back on a time in 1991. My life was in shambles and I had no solution. I began to seek God's help one Sunday morning (September 1, 1991). I remember vividly my situation and condition. I was coming off alcohol and drugs and found myself in a shelter (the George Shinn shelter in uptown Charlotte NC). I had to find someone that could surly help me. For at about thirty I had found my low point; feeling Hopeless and physically helpless (mind and soul). I tell you, experience is truly the best teacher.

The bus from a church (Victory Christian Center) across town came to the shelter that morning and I decided to go along. The pastor's last name was Gool. As I sat there I begin to realize the beauty of the church and was overwhelmed at what God had established in Rev. Gool. And to this day I will always believe I was witnessing the true glory of God. I said to myself, if heaven is anything like this; I want to go. In those few moments I believe my quest to learn more about

God began. After the service I went forth for the alter call. Then I was taken to a room and given more instructions as to how to seek God. I eagerly responded and participated. I left the group feeling hopeful and returned to the shelter.

I couldn't forget what I had witnessed at that church (I will always appreciate the people that helped me that day and today I say to that church, Thank you). I sit down at a desk and with the Bible before me; I began to talk to my inner man. I said, Lord I want to know why my life has come to this point; and I know that the book before me is the only known truth to my knowledge of the existence of mankind (Woman/Man). I wanted to know what was wrong with my life.

From that day I began at the beginning and read through the entire bible. It took me about seven or eight months to complete (reading almost daily). Since that day I have read the bible completely through twice and studied the New Testament more times than I could ever count.

I left the shelter after a few days. I went with some guys that came to the shelter for workers. They said; they had some work in Raleigh NC picking up sweet potatoes or picking tobacco. The work was to pay seventy-five dollars a day. I went for it and by faith I left with them (complete strangers). When we finally got to this place (Fuquay varina NC), which is several miles just outside of Raleigh NC. I was immediately disappointed beyond understanding. The place was seemingly miles back in the woods. The filth and stench of the living quarters was unbelievable. A large group of black people (20 to 30) and one Indian was living on a rundown camp; picking sweet potatoes and tobacco. It reminded me of the slavery days as told in books and movies. I could not believe (black people) were still living like this in our country (USA). My Gosh, it was 1991. (I believe to this day that these camps still operate). These people were working merely for free. A card was given out at the beginning of the week that had one-hundred and ninety dollars credit and whatever was spent from this card was deducted at the end of the week. The stores were several miles away, so they had a trailer set up on the camp that offered an array of products. This trailer offered everything from white liquor, beer, wine, and crack cocaine. I could not believe it. I couldn't believe that my own people were still living as though slavery never happened. It was the worst and most dangerous situation I had put myself in thus far in my life. I was four-hundred miles from home and seemingly had no way out of a senseless situation. I only knew that somewhere inside of me, God was with me.

I stayed at this disgusting place for one day and a half. Because, I knew that there was no way I could stay there under those conditions. The day I went out to work on a rundown school bus to work the fields (the stench of liquor and beer on the bus was breath taking) was my breaking point. I didn't do much work; I could only observe the scene when we got to the fields and shake my head. The scene was unreal. These people were racing to fill up their basket with sweet potatoes and racing back to the truck to dump them; picking up a twenty cent ticket for every bushel they dumped. That's how they were paid. I was numb from head to toe as I observed the chaos. I said to myself, what have I gotten myself into? And that started my mind racing toward a way to get out.

The day in the fields was exhausting and that night I began to figure my way out. In my thinking I doubted that they would take me back to Charlotte and if they knew I wanted out so soon that they might try to kill me. I didn't know what they might do or say to me. Therefore, later that night I gathered my things and told the guys in the room where we slept (six guys in a small room sleeping on military cots) that I was going to air out my cloths. I stepped outside and slowly started walking up the long dirt road; never looking back. I began to get scared that they would notice I was gone and start looking for me (just like in the slavery days). I finally drowned my fears and continued on through the total darkness.

I walked seemingly for miles; hiding in the side ditch when a car would come my way. There was no way I was going back to that camp. I walked until I was exhausted; getting lost. I eventually sought the North Star and followed it (I always heard that if you are lost you can find this star and it will always lead you to civilization). I never knew for certain if I really found the right star; all I know is that I picked one and followed it. I came to a major highway after hours of walking and I was truly relieved. I went across the highway and found a grove of small pine trees that had plenty of pine needles under them and I made a place to sleep. When I lied down I had to laugh to myself and said like the cowboys said back in the western days; I will move out at first light. The next day I moved on and eventually got to the city of Raleigh NC. I believe I was the happiest man on earth when I got there. And to this day I rarely eat sweet potatoes.

The reason I have spoken of this terrible ordeal is because I wanted you to know how I truly found Jesus Christ and how I began my studies into the "Holy Bible". Since that day September I, 1991 I have read the bible completely through twice. I found in my studies that you can search the world over for happiness, but if you are not grounded in the belief that Jesus Christ is the author and finisher of the destination of your soul; then your search will always be for nothing. And there is no one that will care for your well being more than Christ.

I have come a long way from my days of troubled times and today I am moving forward. Moving forward toward the goals and achievements that God has planned for me. Therefore, I tell you; keep your head up no matter your situation right now. It will get better if *YOU* believe in the Almighty. I can't die for your sins and you can't die for mine. Remember also, the key to unlock the door to happiness and respect is humbleness and faith in the Lord. And all the desires of your heart (materialistic things) will follow.

Chapter 12
The Storm is Calm

Life propels itself too swiftly for the concerns of yesterday. Today is here; progress with what your mind and heart can produce herein.

Quote by: Terry Lee McClain

I have written this book with hope in my heart. And my hope is that you may see from my past experiences that there is a better way to live. No matter what you are dealing with *right now*; things can and will get better (if you only believe). There are more miracles happening every day than Matel has toys. Believe me, your situation is not at the worst point if you still have breath in your body and no matter your condition or predicament right now; believe in yourself and the Lord and I guarantee you your situation will change. Trust me, I have been there and done that. If you are on drugs and alcohol (get help for you and not for anyone else), if it is domestic abuse Ladies/men (get out), and if it is relationship problems (broken hearted) Pray. If your situation is financial (hang on and wait on the Lord) your break is right around the corner. I tell you, the above will always work for you if you believe in *yourself* strong enough and have the *desire* in your heart and mind to continue on and see your situation get better.

I have likened my past to that of a boat that sailed out to sea. Many storms came and battered the boat. Somehow (by the Grace and Mercy of God) the boat sailed on. The boat finally came back to the docks and the flag (that read *Hope*) was shredded. The Captain stepped from the boat (seemingly beaten and defeated) and tied it to the docks. He stood on the dock and looked back at the sea; sighed from weariness and said, the Storm is Calm.

Truly, for me today; the storm is calm. Inside my heart and soul (as I speak) the storm is calm. I fully believe that the terrible days lived of my past are gone. I am free inside for the remainder of my life.

My plans to return to school have been delayed since I spoke of it in my first book called "I Hunt" (I will return though) and I still plan to marry my current fiancée (Deneen). I feel blissful inside about my life today; I am free (not in jail or prison), I take my grand-daughter to the McDonald's play pin and to a park when I get her (she loves to play at McDonald's and loves the out of doors), my son and I have a great relationship that can't be measured in worth, my mother (Sally) is doing well at seventy, all six of my brothers are still living and have respectable jobs. My primary family (Ross and McClain) have been truly blessed that our family have not been struck by major tragedies (no missing children, plane crashes, car wrecks, or brutal murders), and my beliefs are truly rooted in Jesus Christ. What more can a man ask for?

I tell you, learn to stop concentrating on the wrongs in your life and look around yourself sometimes and view the world of good that is happening in your life and around you. And I can assure you that you will see the beauty of the blessings of God. You know, Jesus ate honey that He would choose the good.

I write these things that you might see your life is in a better state than you have previously thought. Hey! Look inside yourself for beautiful things and beautiful things will appear outside of you. Happiness is inside you and all around you and yet people are always searching for it. Happiness is only a good thought away.

See, I am still defeating the odds of man (for my beliefs in Christ run deeper than an oil well) because, in 2006 I suffered a heart attack and the doctor told me that if I didn't stop smoking cigarettes I would not see the age of fifty-one. Hey! Glory to God; if it is God's will I will be fifty-one in three more days. And I have been smoking since I left the hospital on August 21, 2006 until this day. I am not promoting smoking cigarettes or bragging about my current health state. I just want you to know in whom I fully put my trust in (the Lord Jesus) and not man. I went to the VA just recently for my yearly check up. I received my lab results from the doctor last week in the mail and everything was normal. I am doing fine.

You cannot continue to worry about what has happened to you in the past. I am here to tell you, that your past was building blocks to get you to the present. I know these things from experience and not from what I have heard.

The odds against you can be defeated. I will give you a few examples. My brother Timmy left the state of NC and traveled to the state of Florida with his wife (Marcheal) and young baby (Ashley) having one-hundred and eighty five dollars to pursue a law degree. And Glory be to God; he secured his degree and is practicing law to this day.

I know another man that turned twenty-one years old on a mental ward and didn't have a direction for his life. Sure enough, today at thirty-six he is Head of Water Treatment for an entire city.

Furthermore, I have a friend (Robert "Pop") that has one of his legs that has little use in it and if you meet this man you would never know that he is limited at his ability to get around. Pop keeps a smile on his face (a true smile) all the time and I have not heard him once complain about his condition and he is seventy-eight years old. Therefore, always know that there is a greater force (positive) working within everyone of us; all you have to do is know in your heart that this force is real and believe in it. And there is almost nothing you can't overcome.

For me, and the rest of the days I live; I know the storm is calm. I know the reality of life today and that makes me happy. Also, I know the other side of reality; that loved ones will die (if I don't go before them) and there is nothing you can do about it. Pray for them that their soul is right with God and mentally absorb reality (we come to earth for a little while); grieve and move on with the rest of your life. Thus, take a good look at your life right now. If you're comfortable with it you're doing well and if you're not; take out some time to look over your past and see just how far God has brought you and change your ways and your thinking and one day you will arise and see a better you.

Therefore, I know what defeating the odds mean and to this day I have nothing to complain about. Through all I have been through (read my first book "I Hunt") and you will know that *faith* weighs more than a ton of gold. Again, I can truly say the storm is calm.

Chapter 13
Learn to Laugh

The one belief I have come to truly believe is that laughter is a tool that can separate a person from reality. I say this because when I laugh I leave from care or concern about health problems, bills, money, and negative feelings.

Therefore, learn to laugh and your happiness will shine like glitter even though it may be a storm over your life. For laughter can and will separate you from the troubles in your life. See, we all should know by now that there is no one perfect and no one lives the perfect life. I have learned to keep it real about my life. I see so many people that put up a smoke screen in front of their lives and behind the screen misery bathes in the sun. I can tell you that even though the storm is calm in my own life; every day is not a brisk walk in the park. I struggle with mismanagement of money and I am not at the status in life I want to obtain.

I really don't want to be rich. For I believe richness is only a highway south to misery. Because, I enjoy taking a walk up town with my girlfriend, going to the grocery store, driving my own vehicle, go fishing, and taking my grand-daughter to the park. My ultimate mission is to be comfortable (financially). I want to reach the point when I have a washing machine go bad; spend several hundred dollars for a new one and go fishing. When the refrigerator goes bad; I have enough money to pay eighteen-hundred dollars for a new one and go on to the beach.

I will never forget the time back in the early 2000's when my brother (Roger) and I was in Florida (supposedly on vacation) visiting our other brother Timmy. We went in a store at Daytona Beach in Florida looking around for some beach towels. We were viewing the prices (seemingly high) and I suddenly realized I was penny pinching on vacation. I leaned over and whispered in my brother's ear. I said, Roger how can we be on vacation when the price of a fifteen-dollar towel scares you half to death? He bent over with laughter and tells me to this day that he learned a valuable lesson from that day. He said later, he knew then that it was time to get his finances in order. And today he really has gotten his finances in order; he just bought a 2008 Cadillac a couple days ago. We both vowed that day that we would see our financial situation change for the better. It was so funny that day. I told my brother, how in the world can you call yourself on vacation and a fifteen- dollar towel send you into convulsions? No way! You're not on vacation; you're just wandering around.

I often focus on times like those and I snap back to reality. The reality of knowing I have to continue keeping my finances in order. I don't have the best financial situation right now, but I am far better off than I was then. I know today that saving money is the best hope of being comfortable or wealthy.

Therefore, always keep moving forward (forget the past and arrange a positive future); because none of us knows just how long we will live. Laugh a little and handle your business too. My goal also is to motivate you to be determined. *Determination* is the key that opens the door to your goals and dreams. Whatever your goals and dreams are; you can reach them. You have to push yourself like pushing through a crowd of people at a college football game.

Like I say, learn to laugh and your mood can change from night to day. I and my brothers laugh among each other often and as I am right now; I feel good within. My life is going very well and I am truly happy.

I really believe I am right at the point in life where I am supposed to be by God's will. Before God, I lie not. You are no different. You too are right where God wants you to be in life (doing good or bad). Trust me. Nothing on this earth right now is out of order. No matter your situation; it is up to you and you alone to alter it. My hopes and prayers are that you will begin to see your life in a new and exciting way. Even through your worst trials and tribulations; think of something good that can bring you relief. It works for me and I don't know a reason why this method of thinking would not work for you. Ask yourself now is my life and my feelings at a point that truly makes me *Happy*? If not then change your situation by believing in your mind that your situation is and will get better. Believe me, your mood about your situation and your life is only a good thought away. My experiences have proven the above to be true. It is not something I heard. I truly believe that a lot of people with aches and pains can feel better by thinking better thoughts in their mind. All in all, the solution to most of your problems *is in your mind.* Therefore, learn to laugh and you will see your situation and your life shine like a new car.

I will give you another situation that I found to be very funny. I called my brother (Roydell "Roy") one day and said, Roy I am coming from the casino and I am broke, if you don't loan me forty dollars I am going to drive my truck off the side of the mountain. Roy said, you better floor it then so you can clear the guard rails; because I ain't got it. I was just joking around with him and he knew it. I even tried to sound serious and it didn't work. We laughed till I was in tears. Like I have stated before, I and my brothers find things to laugh at often and we enjoy ourselves each and every time we get together or talk on the phone.

I may not be a comedian, but I can really make you laugh if you will let me. I don't know a lot of jokes either; but I can guarantee you that if you stay in my presence long enough I will make you laugh.

Chapter 14
Stand Tall

I stand tall today, because I have defeated my past and headed in the right direction for my future. I know though that it is not all about me. My focus in this book is that you may look forward toward *hope.* Hope for a better position for your life. I speak to the young, aging, and old. As long as you have breath in your body; there is hope. Again, I stand tall today because of hope. I never gave in to failure or defeat. I and my brothers were athletes during our youth and we know how to compete. We eat, sleep, and take our next breath for a challenge. We thrive on wins and losses. I tell you, you are a winner. I have moved all around the USA and I have been through some rough times. I mean, I have been through the bottom and yet, I still live and have my being. You can feel the same if you take a good look back at your life and see just how far you have come. See, I know about the troubles and frustrations of this life. And I am telling you, you can overcome your present situation. Even if you are doing fine; there is always room for more relief and comfort. No matter your position right now; your situation can get better.

I remember a time when I had no direction for my life. Believe me, it is not a good feeling. When you hope the next day doesn't come. You know your life is in shambles. I never gave up though (completely). I kept on through all the confusion going on in my life. I am speaking experience to you and I am telling you; you must never completely give up on yourself or your situation. I gather all my strength to function from the (Holly Bible). I will come from St. John 16: 32- 33. It says, Behold, the hour cometh, yea, is now come, that ye shall be scattered, every man to his own, and shall leave me alone: and yet I am not alone, because the Father is with me. These things I have spoken unto you, that in me ye might have peace. In the world ye shall have tribulation: *but be of good cheer; I have overcome the world…* Coming from (Authorized King James Version). See, I feel like if Jesus overcame the world; then there is almost nothing I cannot overcome. You can overcome also. You cannot just talk about it; you have to be about it. I write these things because I know there is something *specific* you are dealing with or going through and you are struggling for a solution. I tell you, you are your solution. No one can help your situation right now but you. Sometimes, you have no one but you and the good Master above. Therefore, take yourself and the Lord and act on helping *yourself.*

I am not speaking as though I live in a rose garden. I am only saying; your help is yourself. Because, no one else knows what you desire to be pleased and no one else knows what it takes to comfort you. I believe that anybody can overcome their situation if they only feel the desire too like feeling sun light upon the skin or a pinch on the arm. Believe me; I have not made it to this point without the help of the Lord and determination within to change the direction of my life. I live a modest life today; free of the general stresses of life, free from worry and frustration. I live west of Charlotte NC in a respectable and quite neighborhood. Mt. Holly NC is a small country type town with a city atmosphere. A working town filled with good hearted people. I love the area and hope to live here a long time to come. I was born in Shelby NC and raised in Kings Mountain NC. I have also lived in Gastonia NC. I like this area because we rarely get bad weather or earthquakes. Hurricane Hugo of 1989 was the strongest of storms to hit this area in many years. I live with my future wife and her two children. My girlfriend and I take a walk uptown every so often and I spend most of my days doing odd jobs for neighbors. I am retired from the Navy and I love to fish. I write because I feel as though I can help someone else and I enjoy it. I just want somebody to see life a different way and not have to go down the road of misery to find a better way to live. I tell you, work hard for what you want for yourself and you will run into happiness along the way. Again, stand tall for yourself and never believe the negative things other people say about you. Don't let anybody tell you that you can't be anything; it is a lie. You can be anything you want to be; you just have to make the right choices. Again, success is only a good choice away. To do wrong is easy, but to do right takes a lot of hard work from within your heart. You have to ask yourself now; do I want life easy or hard? Ask yourself where am I going and how do I get there? See, I have been down the road of heart ache and pain. I want you to choose another path. Believe me; you can lead a better life if you believe in yourself strong enough.

I have come to the point in my life (age fifty-one) that I feel as though the rest of my days on earth will be fine. The great storms of my past are gone and I believe they will not return. Truly, I know the storm is calm. I look at the rest of my life like that of JOB in the Holy Bible; I believe in my soul that God has put a hedge around me as spoken of in the book of JOB chapter 1: 9-10. And I will keep this belief to the death of me. See, through all of my studies of the Bible; I know that the devil cannot do anything to me/you except he ask God. Read JOB and see for yourself. A lot of people know nothing of this mystery; they assume that is Satan causing all the problems in their lives and in fact; it is God sending Satan into your life that you may *believe* and *depend* on Jesus Christ. I am revealing these things because it is in my heart and I have compassion for the outcome of your life. Again, I am not a saint; I truly believe in the Father, the Son, and the Holy Ghost though. Therefore, live your life as though you live in paradise; because you are in paradise if you open your eyes and your mind. Begin to enjoy the beauty and pleasures of life that is at your front door. Your happiness is all around and within you. Hey! These are things you don't have to look far off for. Everything you need to be happy in your life is all around you right now. Thus, stand tall, keep your head up, and keep it moving.

Chapter 15
No Turning Back

Time is in motion and there is no reversing it. Therefore, look into the future with confidence. There is no turning back. I have come too far to turn back now and so have you. I thank my mother (Sally Ann Ross-Mcclain) for everything she has done for me thus far. She worked in factories for many years for less than six dollars an hour to raise seven boys and never once did she leave us to be raised by anyone else. Even through her worst trials and tribulations; she stuck to us like Elmer's glue. She always cooked for us and bathed us. And we always had a clean house to live in. Moma loves to clean up to this day. She is a widow now and lives alone in a modest three bed room home. I can never say that my up bring was bad. I was never abused or neglected by my mother. She treated all of her children the same. My deddy (Robbie Lee McClain) was a hard down to earth working man. He worked hard until his death in 1999. He also hung in there with me and my other brothers. He also had his own trials and tribulations. I thank them both for setting a good example for me to follow with my own life. Again, I can say to my mother, *Thank You* and I will love you always.

Again, I believe the last state of a man/woman is their best testimony. No matter what your past was like; you can still leave a good example of your life for someone else to lead by. My deddy left the example that if you work hard and be determined; you can accomplish anything you want to. And you can have whatever your heart desires (materialistic).

I have said the above to let you know that I have come from a long way to be where I am today. And I have had a lot of help along the way. I say to the young; never forget where you came from. Always remember who helped you along. Some people get to the top of their success ladder and forget that they had help along the way. I don't care who you are or how high you climb the success ladder; somebody helped you get there. Either God or another human helped you get to where you are and there is no way around this *fact*. Today, people want to put themselves in classes (wanting to seem better than others). I tell you, we are all the same and that is how I view every man/woman. A BMW will get you to the same destination as a KIA. Cars don't make people; people make cars. I say the above to let you know that the suit don't make the man/woman; the man/woman makes the suit. See, I come from two bed room houses occupied by eight people. I worked many years in cotton mills, ran the streets like a lost puppy, and spent time in jail & prison. Today, I am retired and bring in a comfortable income. And I believe I am no different than the man at the intersection holding up a homeless sign. I am saying; no one knows what you can eventually be. Ask president Obama. You can be whatever you want to be in America. Therefore, look not down on a man/woman because of their past; because you have one too. I tell you, you can't turn back now.

I look at my uncle (Bobby) who was once driven by the ways of the world. Today he is an aspiring actor of biblical material and I have not seen too many actors better than him. I am serious; I am praying for him each and every day that he fulfill his dream. He is an exceptional play writer from Shelby NC. Therefore, we never know what the last state of a person can be.

I am moving forward with the plans and ideas I continue to follow. Truly, I plan to return to college at UNC-Charlotte this fall or the next winter. I also plan to buy a new house soon (one of my dreams for many years now) and marry my present *Queen*. She has been a world of *Help* to me financially and mentally. She is very supportive of nearly everything I attempt. I must do well in life for my four year old grand-daughter (Ariah); she is now the catalyst toward all my attempts to lead a respectable life. I lie not. Therefore, I know there is no turning back for me. For I believe it's not all about me or where I came from; where I go from here is all that matters to me. Also, I believe it not about where you come from, but where you end up. Again, the last state of a man/woman is the best testimony.

I say to you, follow your dreams to the best of your ability. If you live in America; anything is possible. But you can make your dreams come true no matter where you are in the world. Make it happen.

I hope you have come to understand my writings and have enjoyed reading this book thus far. My ultimate goal at writing this book is to let you know that your problems, worries, and frustrations can be over if you begin to believe in yourself and the good Lord. Many of your struggles, headaches, and troubles will disappear and you can begin a new life and new way of living. I hope you have learned from my past experiences that there is a better path to choose. I tell you (young people); lead and live a good life and you will save yourself a lot of heartaches and headaches. I cater to the young because I see so many today that really don't have a direction for their life. I say to them; go to school and get your education, obtain a good paying career, and set positive standards for yourself. You do not have to live your life out like you see of the negative minded people around you or in your life right now. You don't have to struggle to make a good living any more. Times are not like the slavery days any more. The opportunity to lead a successful life is in the palm of your hands. Use your mind to do work for you. And for the love of God; stop killing yourselves. Suicide is never the answer to your problems; always talk out to somebody as to what you are dealing with. Talk to a perfect stranger if that is what it takes. Please, get help. Help is only available if you ask for it. Because, nobody knows what is going on in your mind but you and you know when something is troubling you. Therefore, learn to get in touch with your true feelings; learn to know when something is going wrong in your body and mind. I know; I have been where you are now. I have been there. So; pray and gather yourself and move on with the *precious gift of life* that God has given you. You are not the only one dealing with an issue; for everybody is dealing with something (big or small). There is not one human being living that doesn't have something they're dealing with. Thus, take some time out right now and clear your thoughts and move on with your life. Like I said, I have lived the above type of moments and got through them. You can get through too. Always know that you are a special gift to mankind and possess special abilities. Find them and use them to the best of your ability and you will see for yourself that I speak no lies.

No turning back. I put my trust in myself and the Lord that I will live a good long life. I wish not for richness; I hope to stay humble and respectful toward my fellow man/woman. And I believe that all the materialistic things (my heart's desire) will come to me.

I have spoken the above that you (if troubled times are upon you) will know that I care for you and your present predicament. And I pray that you will see your way through. For you are all you have. I have found that in the worst moments of despair; I had no one but myself.

See, these are some of the worst of troubled times. There are so many temptations. Scams, guns, alcohol, drugs, strip clubs, internet dating, and sex. It is not easy to stay clear of all these temptations. Just know your limit and look closely at what you're getting involved in. I have learned to stay clear of nearly all the above. Like I have said though, we all have some kind of affection for something. I have my faults also. I acknowledge my faults and deal with them one by one. I try not to indulge in too many things at once. That is how I stay clear of temptations. I know for sure within what is good for me and what is not. I have learned to discern good from evil. I have been sober for over three years now and I tell you; if you can get away from excessive drinking (alcohol) then your chances of indulging in other sinful activities are lessened. I am saying; alcohol is the gate you travel through to get to many more sinful acts. Believe me or not.

I speak the above from experience. I wish for you not to travel down some of the roads I have. They will defeat you. This book is my warning to you and I hope and pray that you will take heed to my writings. Jail, prison, institutions (mental), and death have no respect for you. They say to you if you don't care then neither do I.

I wish to switch gears. I want my grand-daughter (Ariah M. McClain) to know that the advice forthcoming is invaluable. See, when I was growing up I never had anyone to talk to me about money. I didn't have anyone to tell me how to control my finances. Therefore, I am telling the young people and my grand-daughter. Learn how to control your money. Save it. As you go through life invest your money into banks and the stock market. They hold a world of wealth. Learn any aspect of money managing and you will enjoy the pleasures that life has to offer. My grand baby is four now and I hope and pray that one day she will be able to appreciate what I have spoken above. I want you and her to know these things because I care for the well being of your future. I want to leave behind a dear legacy; a life lasting legacy that I have done my very best to show somebody a better way to carry out their days in life. I don't plan on leaving this world any time soon, but I know one day I must go. I accept the reality of that fact. I want my son (Philip A. McClain) also to know that as a parent, I did my very best to be there for you growing up. I truly love you both. And I am ecstatic that they are a part of my life today.

See, time is the healer of all pain. Therefore, mothers; never leave your children no matter your circumstance. You can make it. I feel that if God allowed you to get pregnant then He intended to take care of you and the baby. I had a great mother and I thank her to this day that she never neglected us. She stood right beside us (my brothers and I) no matter what her and my deddy was dealing with. I tell you, there is no greater love on earth than that of a true mother. It is such a good feeling as a grown up too know that your mother took care of you. Thus, women; take care of your children no matter what. And if you have a man that doesn't want to help you; GET RID OF HIM. Ladies, don't mess up your life for some dude that is not helping you take care of your children. Don't continue wasting your time. Move on with your life with your children. No matter the cost. Like I have said before; I will die for a cause I believe in strong enough. Ladies, all I am saying is that you don't have to live with an abusive man. Love can run deep, but it is not worth a black eye or busted lip. Having real love for somebody doesn't mean doing physical harm to them. That is just the way I see it.

I now want to thank everyone who has helped me along in some kind of way; especially my mother (Sally), Deneen, Jack, "Flip", Julius, Stevie, James, "Woody" (of whom stuck by me through thick and thin when I was trying to get my benefits from the VA), Buck, Danny and his wife Linda, and my brother Lance. And if I forgot to mention anybody else, I mean no disrespect. But the above people I do consider my true friends. These people have an understanding heart. I can talk to them no matter if my circumstance is good or bad. Again, I say; thank you.

Chapter 16
Hope

My hope is that you have enjoyed reading my book thus far. I hope that you have read something profound and can put it into your life. I tell you; sometimes all you have to lean on is *Hope*. To this day I still live by the hope I once read about in a book called "A Nickles Worth of Hope" by Andrea Vandenberg. I strongly suggest you read it. You can order it online from Books-A-Million. If you really want to know what hope really means then read this book. I read it thoroughly many years ago and I keep its meaning dear within my heart to this day.

Hope to me is more precious than all the gold, diamonds, and pearls in the world. It has been a treasure to me.

I said the above to let you know that I have hope for you. I hope that you will see better days in the future. I hope that by you reading this book you will begin with confidence and build your determination. Build your determination to its greatest height. For I believe determination is a key to the locked door of success, happiness, and material wealth. Having good sense helps a lot too. Therefore, remember *always* that I am pulling for you. I am your friend and I hope the best for you. I have written this book from my heart and truthful experience. Take what you have read and use it to the best of your ability and I guarantee you will see your life change and your situation get better. I am not a magician, special healer, know it all, or God. I am just a country boy (as people say) and I am just trying to make the best of a life given to me by God. Therefore, I tell you; there is no magic formula to happiness and prosperity. You just got to believe in something (God, a pack of peanuts, or a six foot tall bunny rabbit) and hope your situation get better. Even at your worst point; keep hope alive! I am telling you; when you have *hope* things happen.

In 2011 I set out on a journey. I needed to go to the veteran's hospital. I was in bad shape and had no one to take me. I began to walk the distance; I was eighty miles from the VA hospital in Salisbury NC. I left Lowell NC one morning and started walking down highway 85 North. I walked to Charlotte NC before I caught a ride of about ten miles. I walked to the other side of Charlotte and rested overnight in some bushes along the highway. The next morning I continued on to the other side of Concord NC and eventually caught another ride into Salisbury. I walked about fifty five of the eighty miles. It took me three days to get to Salisbury overall. I was accepted into the hospital and eventually received full benefits. Therefore, *hope* was the only thing I had to lean on during that three day journey. That's why I said earlier; when you *hope* for something things happens. I have had many situations where hope pulled me through. I tell you; stop believing that the devil is working in and around your life. The devil cannot do anything to you except he ask God. Again, read the book of JOB- first chapter and if you believe in what is written in the bible; then you will know for yourself that it is not the devil working in your life. It is God trying to get your attention. Again, if you are going to get your life back on track; have faith and keep hope in your heart, mind, and soul.

I thank you in the deepest depths of my heart for taking time out to read this book. I will always pray for you and hope this book has been a help to you. Also, I hope from my experiences you will see a light at the end of your dark tunnel. And if things are going well for you then I am happy for you and continue the good fight. I hope I have been a light into your path through life.

At age fifty- one as of June 18, 2014 I have overcome some of the greatest odds against me. I go into the future now with complete confidence and determination. I see brighter days ahead. I pray that you will see brighter days also. I tend to set back often and absorb the beauty of existence and peace in my heart. Again, the storm is calm. I lie down at night with joy in my soul; knowing I have done my very best for that day. I always pray in the morning for the blessings of the day from God and acknowledge at the end of the day that whatever happened from morning till I go back to bed at night; I was in the will of God. I don't look at my life any other way. For I believe that everything that occurs in a day is the will of God (good or bad). My hope is also that you will perceive from reading this book as to what we are dealing with when it comes to God. I know what I am dealing with. Because I know that the moment I lay down my faith; something not pleasing to me will happen. I tell you; there is a greater force working in earth than you and I can imagine. I call this force the *Power of God.* Believe me or not. I truly believe in this force and hope that you will begin to have confidence that this force will take care of you too.

Chapter 17

Freedom

Independence Day (4th of July) is close to come and I feel good that it is drawing near. I can feel the energy now. Out of all the holidays of a year; the 4th of July is my favorite. It means freedom and truly in my spirit; I know I am free. I know a lot of my ancestors gave their lives in order for me to be free. I acknowledge every one of them right now and say, *Thank you.* I thank them for the ultimate sacrifice; to lay down their lives for a cause. Sometimes, you have to feel reality and know that it was a price paid for you and me to be free. I tell you; I would not trade my freedom for all the jewels in the world. I will have a moment of silence for these people on that day.

Freedom means to me that there are no restrictions on my goings and comings. I can go almost anywhere I choose to go. I can be in church and recognize just how free I am. I have spent days in bondage and not one of them was comfortable. I know how caged in animals feel and I sympathize for them. I do know too that some of these animals are wild and ferocious and must be caged.

That is just reality. Even so, I love my freedom and hope to keep it the rest of my life. I hope you can absorb the same feeling as I and have a wonderful 4th of July. And if you are in a place where your freedom is restricted; pray and *never* give up that you too will one day be free. I tell you; I feel like the very beauty of watching fireworks explode. I am at ease. I am looking forward to spending that day with my son and grand-daughter and a small group of other family members and friends. Wow! I can taste the grilled out food now. There is no better taste than grilled out food. And if your independence day is not like the USA then whatever day yours in on; enjoy it and be safe. A world of fun can happen on this day if you be safe; and please don't drink (alcohol) and drive. Remember, perhaps your job and your freedom can be lost if *you* choose to drink and drive. People, it is not worth it.

Also, I can't forget how free I felt last weekend when me and my grand-daughter was at the park. I looked back at the days of troubled times and realized how good it feels to be free. Free from major stress, free from worry, concern, and frustrations. I tell you; it is an exhilarating feeling that is worth more than a mine full of gold.

Therefore, take some time now and relax your mind and absorb the free feeling I speak of and you will release a sigh of relief and relieve yourself of a ton of pressure.

Chapter 18
Closing

I have written this book for you and I have given you my deepest thoughts and inner most feelings. I hope you can take what you have read and use it as a tool to carve out a better life for yourself. Know that you are a king or a queen and I know that you have the ability to live a good (productive) life. I have all the confidence in the world in you.

My primary purpose for writing is that I know there is someone in the world that needs somebody to talk to them. I just want to save at least one person from going down the same path as I did; the path that caused me so many heartaches (jail, prison, wandering the streets, drinking excessively, and doing drugs). I have been disappointed about myself so many times in the past. I have been where you may be right now and I am telling you from my heart. Stop right now or for the next few moments or the next few minutes; however long it has to take. Gather yourself and say, it's alright now. It's going to work for you. Soon, time will allow you to heal or help get you through your worst times of troubles. Basically, shake yourself and say, get yourself together. Believe me, it works. I would not be writing to you now if I would have lied down years ago and just gave up. I would not be speaking to you right now. I believe in you as I do myself, but you have to want to help yourself first. I am mostly speaking to the young people of our society. To the older group I say; you are never going to be old enough that you can't learn something from a younger person. I have learned things from young and old and I am not afraid to learn more from someone else. See, I don't claim I know everything as some people do. Like I have said, experience has learned me the most. I believe that you can't relate to someone unless you have been in a similar predicament. You can't tell me about jail if you have never been there. I just don't see the relation. And there are many more situations I can describe.

I am almost sure that the problem with most people is themselves. Yea, as I am a lot of times; I am my biggest problem. And I am sure you can relate to this. See, everything about living doesn't come with instructions in a neat little package that you can pick up at a local convenience store. Sometimes you have to let somebody show you a better way. I have not painted you a pretty picture in this book and live my life in misery. I have kept it real and know that the things I have spoken of throughout this story are reality and have been real experiences.

Therefore, I am closing with this; always know that I adore you with compassion and I will never wish the worst for you. I hope that we meet one day and you tell me that this book had an impact in your life. I also have faith that one day you will be happy as a new bride. Again, take what you have learned and use it. By reading this book you're already one step closer to where you want to be. Get you for a change! Believe that it is your time to shine. For me, I know that I have overcome and I am truly moving forward with joy and confidence. I don't see living my life any different from here on. In closing, I ask you to continue to pray for me. For we all need prayer; no matter if you're doing good or bad. I know I need somebody to always pray for me. Like I have said throughout this book; I am not where I want to be (yet), but I thank the Lord I am not where I used to be. It is a good feeling to know within yourself that you're doing fine. And to know that the next breath you take it is getting better. The storm is calm I tell you.

I hope you have enjoyed this story and will keep the experience of reading it dear to your heart. I have thoroughly enjoyed writing to you and for you. I hope my writings have and will make a difference in your life. Again, I am always for you; even if you have no one else on your side. I pump my fist for you, because if not already; soon you will see that I have spoken to you the truth. I have given you the best of what I know about life and I pray that it will be a world of help to you. I am not proud of my past and there is nothing heroic about it. I know today that those were days I had to go through to get to the better days I live now. And I believe that it was all purposed by God. For I truly believe that there is nothing going on right now in the world that is out of order. Everything is just as God wants it to be. Therefore, I am telling you; you are not out of place. You are right where God wants you to be no matter your situation or predicament. It is up to you to change your position. Again; like I have heard, when you are driving a car down the road and let go of the steering wheel; God is not going to grab the steering wheel and drive the car for you. You will crash! I bet you. See, God left it up to us to sometimes use our common sense. Even now if you are not where you want to be with your life; then thoroughly look at your present circumstance and judge if it's good or bad, then use some common sense to seek a solution to your predicament. Look, sleeping under a bridge or holding up a homeless sign at an intersection is not using good common sense; it is not going to change your situation much. Getting in touch with the people that can help you; that is using common sense. Like I said, sometimes it is you that is your problem and not God. A lot of people want to blame God for their predicament and never once consider that the problem might be with them (themselves). Sometimes people ought to praise God for not being in a worst predicament. I know I do. Again, it's up to you as to what happens to you. If you want misery then there is enough to go around. And if you want better for yourself then go for it. Hey! This is America. Anything can happen and I mean anything. You can be through the bottom one day and the next day you can be cruising on a pontoon boat. That is just how fast it can happen.

Opportunity is not going to come and jump up on your lap like a cat. I am just saying; if you want something bad enough you have to move to get it. Pleasure is not going to sneak up on you and grab you by the throat. And happiness is never going to be delivered to your door like a pizza.

I have to mention my son (Philip A. McClain "META#4) who works full time and baby sits his daughter and has launched a music career as a singer and song writer of rap material. His new album called P.O.V. was released on

June 5th 2014 and I know it will do well. Ask him if any of his determination to go get it came and jumped in his lap?

My fiancée has worked full time for the same company for over fifteen years and during ten of those years she worked part-time for a department store; and raised three children. Ask her if her determination came and snatched her by the arm and said, come on? The answer will be no; you have to go out and get it.

All I am saying is that nothing good that you want is going to break in your house at night while you are sleeping and snatch you out of bed. You got to go out there in the world and get what you want. There is plenty of prosperity to be shared. I say it this way; if you keep waiting on an opportunity to come and get you; then keep waiting and soon somebody will be coming to your wake.

Finally, I wish you well at your new direction in life and I hope one day soon you too will be able to say, the storm is calm. Farewell. Author, Terry Lee McClain (June 24th 2014).

Continue to pray for me as I do for you and all others.

ACKNOWLEDGEMENTS

I thank the Lord first for the blessings he has bestowed upon my life and I am forever thankful. To my fiancée (Deneen), my mother (Sally), my brothers (Roydell, Lance, and Roger) of whom I have had many serious and helpful conversations with, my son (Philip Austin McClain "META#4") and my grand-daughter (Ariah Melody McClain) of whom I am so proud of them both and I want them to know that I love them forever and ever, and friends and other family members. And Gerome Parker of whom suggested I say more about the old days in Ebenezer in this book. Again, thank you for all that you have done for me.